BIG BOOK
of
Disney
SONGS

T0039546

Available for
FLUTE, CLARINET, ALTO SAX, TENOR SAX, TRUMPET,
HORN, TROMBONE, VIOLIN, VIOLA, CELLO

ISBN 978-1-4584-1133-4

Walt Disney Music Company
Wonderland Music Company, Inc.

DISTRIBUTED BY

HAL•LEONARD®
CORPORATION

7777 W. BLUEMOUND RD. P.O. BOX 13819 MILWAUKEE, WI 53213

In Australia Contact:
Hal Leonard Australia Pty. Ltd.
4 Lentara Court
Cheltenham, Victoria, 3192 Australia
Email: ausadmin@halleonard.com.au

Visit Hal Leonard Online at
www.halleonard.com

CONTENTS

ALICE IN WONDERLAND
from Walt Disney's ALICE IN WONDERLAND

ALTO SAX

Words by BOB HILLIARD
Music by SAMMY FAIN

THE BALLAD OF DAVY CROCKETT
from Walt Disney's DAVY CROCKETT

Words by TOM BLACKBURN
Music by GEORGE BRUNS

BE OUR GUEST
from Walt Disney's BEAUTY AND THE BEAST

Lyrics by HOWARD ASHMAN
Music by ALAN MENKEN

Moderately

THE BARE NECESSITIES

from Walt Disney's THE JUNGLE BOOK

ALTO SAX

Words and Music by
TERRY GILKYSON

BEAUTY AND THE BEAST

from Walt Disney's BEAUTY AND THE BEAST

ALTO SAX

Lyrics by HOWARD ASHMAN
Music by ALAN MENKEN

ALTO SAX

BELLA NOTTE
(This Is the Night)
from Walt Disney's LADY AND THE TRAMP

Words and Music by PEGGY LEE
and SONNY BURKE

BIBBIDI-BOBBIDI-BOO
(The Magic Song)
from Walt Disney's CINDERELLA

Words by JERRY LIVINGSTON
Music by MACK DAVID and AL HOFFMAN

CRUELLA DE VIL

from Walt Disney's 101 DALMATIANS

Words and Music by
MEL LEVEN

BREAKING FREE

ALTO SAX

from the Disney Channel Original Movie HIGH SCHOOL MUSICAL

Words and Music by
JAMIE HOUSTON

BEST OF FRIENDS

from Walt Disney's THE FOX AND THE HOUND

ALTO SAX

Words by STAN FIDEL
Music by RICHARD JOHNSTON

CAN YOU FEEL THE LOVE TONIGHT

from Walt Disney Pictures' THE LION KING

ALTO SAX

Music by ELTON JOHN
Lyrics by TIM RICE

Pop Ballad

14

CANDLE ON THE WATER

from Walt Disney's PETE'S DRAGON

ALTO SAX

Words and Music by AL KASHA
and JOEL HIRSCHHORN

CHIM CHIM CHER-EE

from Walt Disney's MARY POPPINS

ALTO SAX

Words and Music by RICHARD M. SHERMAN
and ROBERT B. SHERMAN

Lightly, with gusto

small notes optional

COLORS OF THE WIND

from Walt Disney's POCAHONTAS

ALTO SAX

Music by ALAN MENKEN
Lyrics by STEPHEN SCHWARTZ

A DREAM IS A WISH YOUR HEART MAKES

from Walt Disney's CINDERELLA

Words and Music by MACK DAVID,
AL HOFFMAN and JERRY LIVINGSTON

CIRCLE OF LIFE
from Walt Disney Pictures' THE LION KING

ALTO SAX

Music by ELTON JOHN
Lyrics by TIM RICE

Moderately (with an African beat)

GO THE DISTANCE

from Walt Disney Pictures' HERCULES

ALTO SAX

Music by ALAN MENKEN
Lyrics by DAVID ZIPPEL

FRIEND LIKE ME

from Walt Disney's ALADDIN

ALTO SAX

Lyrics by HOWARD ASHMAN
Music by ALAN MENKEN

GOD HELP THE OUTCASTS
from Walt Disney's THE HUNCHBACK OF NOTRE DAME

ALTO SAX

Music by ALAN MENKEN
Lyrics by STEPHEN SCHWARTZ

HOW D'YE DO AND SHAKE HANDS

from Walt Disney's ALICE IN WONDERLAND

Words by CY COBEN
Music by OLIVER WALLACE

HAKUNA MATATA
from Walt Disney Pictures' THE LION KING

ALTO SAX

Music by ELTON JOHN
Lyrics by TIM RICE

HE'S A TRAMP
from Walt Disney's LADY AND THE TRAMP

Words and Music by PEGGY LEE
and SONNY BURKE

I JUST CAN'T WAIT TO BE KING

from Walt Disney Pictures' THE LION KING

ALTO SAX

Music by ELTON JOHN
Lyrics by TIM RICE

I'M LATE
from Walt Disney's ALICE IN WONDERLAND

Words by BOB HILLIARD
Music by SAMMY FAIN

IF I NEVER KNEW YOU
(Love Theme from POCAHONTAS)
from Walt Disney's POCAHONTAS

ALTO SAX

Music by ALAN MENKEN
Lyrics by STEPHEN SCHWARTZ

IT'S A SMALL WORLD

from Disneyland Resort® and Magic Kingdom® Park

ALTO SAX

Words and Music by RICHARD M. SHERMAN
and ROBERT B. SHERMAN

LAVENDER BLUE

(Dilly Dilly)

from Walt Disney's SO DEAR TO MY HEART

Words by LARRY MOREY
Music by ELIOT DANIEL

LET'S GET TOGETHER

from Walt Disney Pictures' THE PARENT TRAP

Words and Music by RICHARD M. SHERMAN
and ROBERT B. SHERMAN

LET'S GO FLY A KITE

from Walt Disney's MARY POPPINS

ALTO SAX

Words and Music by RICHARD M. SHERMAN
and ROBERT B. SHERMAN

MY FUNNY FRIEND AND ME

from Walt Disney Pictures' THE EMPEROR'S NEW GROOVE

Lyrics by STING
Music by STING and DAVID HARTLEY

LITTLE APRIL SHOWER

from Walt Disney's BAMBI

ALTO SAX

Words by LARRY MOREY
Music by FRANK CHURCHILL

THE LORD IS GOOD TO ME

from Walt Disney's MELODY TIME
from Walt Disney's JOHNNY APPLESEED

Words and Music by KIM GANNON
and WALTER KENT

MICKEY MOUSE MARCH

from Walt Disney's THE MICKEY MOUSE CLUB

Words and Music by
JIMMIE DODD

KISS THE GIRL

from Walt Disney's THE LITTLE MERMAID

ALTO SAX

Music by ALAN MENKEN
Lyrics by HOWARD ASHMAN

NEVER SMILE AT A CROCODILE

from Walt Disney's PETER PAN

ALTO SAX

Words by JACK LAWRENCE
Music by FRANK CHURCHILL

PART OF YOUR WORLD

from Walt Disney's THE LITTLE MERMAID

ALTO SAX

Music by ALAN MENKEN
Lyrics by HOWARD ASHMAN

ONCE UPON A DREAM
from Walt Disney's SLEEPING BEAUTY

ALTO SAX

Words and Music by SAMMY FAIN
and JACK LAWRENCE
Adapted from a Theme by Tchaikovsky

REFLECTION
from Walt Disney Pictures' MULAN

Music by MATTHEW WILDER
Lyrics by DAVID ZIPPEL

A PIRATE'S LIFE
from Walt Disney's PETER PAN

ALTO SAX

Words by ED PENNER
Music by OLIVER WALLACE

SCALES AND ARPEGGIOS
from Walt Disney's THE ARISTOCATS

Words and Music by RICHARD M. SHERMAN
and ROBERT B. SHERMAN

THE SECOND STAR TO THE RIGHT

from Walt Disney's PETER PAN

Words by SAMMY CAHN
Music by SAMMY FAIN

SALUDOS AMIGOS

from Walt Disney's SALUDOS AMIGOS
from Walt Disney's THE THREE CABALLEROS

ALTO SAX

Words by NED WASHINGTON
Music by CHARLES WOLCOTT

SO THIS IS LOVE
(The Cinderella Waltz)
from Walt Disney's CINDERELLA

ALTO SAX

Words and Music by MACK DAVID,
AL HOFFMAN and JERRY LIVINGSTON

THE SIAMESE CAT SONG

from Walt Disney's LADY AND THE TRAMP

ALTO SAX

Words and Music by PEGGY LEE
and SONNY BURKE

SOONER OR LATER

from Walt Disney's SONG OF THE SOUTH

Words and Music by RAY GILBERT
and CHARLES WOLCOTT

(knock, knock)

(knock, knock)

SOMEDAY

from Walt Disney's THE HUNCHBACK OF NOTRE DAME

ALTO SAX

Music by ALAN MENKEN
Lyrics by STEPHEN SCHWARTZ

SOMEONE'S WAITING FOR YOU

from Walt Disney's THE RESCUERS

ALTO SAX

Words by CAROL CONNORS and AYN ROBBINS
Music by SAMMY FAIN

A SPOONFUL OF SUGAR

from Walt Disney's MARY POPPINS

ALTO SAX

Words and Music by RICHARD M. SHERMAN
and ROBERT B. SHERMAN

THESE ARE THE BEST TIMES
from Walt Disney Productions' SUPERDAD

ALTO SAX

Words and Music by
SHANE TATUM

SWEET SURRENDER

from Walt Disney's THE BEARS AND I

ALTO SAX

Words and Music by
JOHN DENVER

TOYLAND MARCH
from Walt Disney's BABES IN TOYLAND

Adapted from V. HERBERT Melody
Words by MEL LEVEN
Music by GEORGE BRUNS

March tempo

TRASHIN' THE CAMP

from Walt Disney Pictures' TARZAN™

ALTO SAX

Words and Music by
PHIL COLLINS

Wooh!

Gradually faster

Wooh!   *Wooh!*

Wooh!   *Wooh!*   *Wooh!*

WESTWARD HO, THE WAGONS!
from Walt Disney's WESTWARD HO, THE WAGONS!

Words by TOM BLACKBURN
Music by GEORGE BRUNS

Lively

SUPERCALIFRAGILISTICEXPIALIDOCIOUS

from Walt Disney's MARY POPPINS

ALTO SAX

Words and Music by RICHARD M. SHERMAN
and ROBERT B. SHERMAN

THE UNBIRTHDAY SONG
from Walt Disney's ALICE IN WONDERLAND

ALTO SAX

Words and Music by MACK DAVID,
AL HOFFMAN and JERRY LIVINGSTON

UNDER THE SEA

from Walt Disney's THE LITTLE MERMAID

ALTO SAX

Music by ALAN MENKEN
Lyrics by HOWARD ASHMAN

WE'RE ALL IN THIS TOGETHER

from the Disney Channel Original Movie HIGH SCHOOL MUSICAL

ALTO SAX

Words and Music by MATTHEW GERRARD
and ROBBIE NEVIL

CODA

WHEN SHE LOVED ME

from Walt Disney Pictures' TOY STORY 2 - A Pixar Film

ALTO SAX

Music and Lyrics by
RANDY NEWMAN

Tenderly, very freely

WINNIE THE POOH

from Walt Disney's THE MANY ADVENTURES OF WINNIE THE POOH

Words and Music by RICHARD M. SHERMAN
and ROBERT B. SHERMAN

Tenderly

WHERE THE DREAM TAKES YOU

from Walt Disney Pictures' ATLANTIS: THE LOST EMPIRE

ALTO SAX

Lyrics by DIANE WARREN
Music by DIANE WARREN
and JAMES NEWTON HOWARD

A WHOLE NEW WORLD

from Walt Disney's ALADDIN

ALTO SAX

Music by ALAN MENKEN
Lyrics by TIM RICE

A WHALE OF A TALE

from Walt Disney's 20,000 LEAGUES UNDER THE SEA

ALTO SAX

Words and Music by NORMAN GIMBEL
and AL HOFFMAN

With a bounce

THE WONDERFUL THING ABOUT TIGGERS

from Walt Disney's THE MANY ADVENTURES OF WINNIE THE POOH

Words and Music by RICHARD M. SHERMAN
and ROBERT B. SHERMAN

Very brightly

YO HO
(A Pirate's Life for Me)
from PIRATES OF THE CARIBBEAN at Disneyland Park and Magic Kingdom Park

Words by XAVIER ATENCIO
Music by GEORGE BRUNS

WRINGLE WRANGLE
(A Pretty Woman's Love)
from Walt Disney's WESTWARD HO, THE WAGONS!

ALTO SAX

Words and Music by
STAN JONES

(whistle) Hey! (slap leg)

(whistle) Hey! (slap leg)

(whistle) Hey! (slap leg)

1.   2.

(whistle) Hey! (slap leg)

WRITTEN IN THE STARS

from Elton John and Tim Rice's AIDA

ALTO SAX

Music by ELTON JOHN
Lyrics by TIM RICE

YOU ARE THE MUSIC IN ME

from the Disney Channel Original Movie HIGH SCHOOL MUSICAL 2

ALTO SAX

Words and Music by
JAMIE HOUSTON

Moderately fast Rock

YOU'LL BE IN MY HEART

(Pop Version)

from Walt Disney Pictures' TARZAN™

ALTO SAX

Words and Music by
PHIL COLLINS

YOU CAN FLY! YOU CAN FLY! YOU CAN FLY!

ALTO SAX

from Walt Disney's PETER PAN

Words by SAMMY CAHN
Music by SAMMY FAIN

YOU'VE GOT A FRIEND IN ME
from Walt Disney's TOY STORY

ALTO SAX

Music and Lyrics by
RANDY NEWMAN

ZERO TO HERO

from Walt Disney Pictures' HERCULES

ALTO SAX

Music by ALAN MENKEN
Lyrics by DAVID ZIPPEL

ZIP-A-DEE-DOO-DAH

from Walt Disney's SONG OF THE SOUTH

ALTO SAX

Words by RAY GILBERT
Music by ALLIE WRUBEL